In her stunning poetry col
deconstructs and reconstr
time and place (Moscow Plains, Michigan, 1885) and
inhabits them so completely, it blurs our sense of the
past and present. The result is a mesmerizing biography-
in-poems of a woman awash in loneliness and isolation
whose salvation is the natural world. This unnamed
woman immerses herself in that world—in the glowing
light of its moon, its pale pink dawn, its milk glass
snow—in order to survive the tragedies of death and
loss. In one of the most powerful poems, two women
(a mother and grown daughter) both grieve their dead
children. Here, there is no barrier between the living
and the dead: the living tend graves and lovingly collect
mementos; the dead hold a bowl of raspberries and burn
through a blizzard straight to God. The book is filled with
these startling images—resonant and nuanced—like
the discovery of a sparrow's nest "made entirely of her
own hair." *She Calls the Moon by Its Name* is a seamless
collection which embraces all that truly matters—life,
death, the resilience of the natural world and the human
spirit. DuPont creates an unforgettable landscape, an
unforgettable persona. They both shimmer and sing.

Linda Nemec Foster
author of *The Blue Divide* and *Bone Country*

She Calls the Moon by Its Name is a sublime journey of
loss, mourning, and renewal.

Faye Moskowitz
essayist, former poetry editor of *Moment,*
and author of *A Leak in the Heart*

Lonnie Hull DuPont's *She Calls the Moon by Its Name* stuns with its quiet acceptance of the constant cohabitation of wonder and grief. In poems created with the unpretentious and sacred elegance of Shaker furniture, DuPont takes us back to the late 1800s and, through the world of "She," gives us one of the great good gifts of authentic art: life as we will never know it. We soon realize we're sitting on the farmhouse front porch listening to the soft-spoken, brave, loving music of plainsong. DuPont's collection is a remarkably refreshing accomplishment of imagination, understanding, intelligence, and artistry enabling us to admire the noble endurance of "She" and those who share her life of unending work both physical and spiritual. As we near the time of the pink moon, we read in a whisper, "She touches his arm./All these years." and we leave wondering what we've lost while we've been assuming that we've gained.

Jack Ridl
author of *Practicing to Walk Like a Heron*,
recipient of the Best Collection of Poetry Award
from ForeWord Reviews

Lonnie Hull DuPont's poems are accessible, engaging, and rich with original imagery. I have heard her read poems from this collection, and the experience was like nothing I've ever heard before. She is a very fine poet.

M. L. Liebler
Award-Winning Detroit Poet and Editor of
RESPECT: Poets in Detroit Music (MSU Press)

She Calls the Moon
by Its Name

Lonnie Hull DuPont

She Calls the Moon by Its Name

©2023 by Lonnie Hull DuPont

Fernwood Press
Newberg, Oregon
www.fernwoodpress.com

Printed in the United States of America

Cover and interior design: Mareesa Fawver Moss
Author photo: lidija A. Fremeau
Cover art: Mary Hertler Tallman (www.MaryHertlerTallmanArt.com)

ISBN 978-1-59498-101-2

to my good friend Clyde McKaney
whose music brings my poetry to life

Contents

Foreword

Growing up, I was dimly aware of Lonnie Hull DuPont, the poet sister of my aunt-by-marriage. Lonnie had bloomed, as I did twenty years later, in the southern Michigan soil where we were both born and raised—each with a penchant for words which unsuited us to the rural working world that surrounded us.

During much of my life, Lonnie was the only writer of whom I personally knew—the shirttail relation who had moved, alone, to Greece, where she taught herself the language (enough to dream in it, as she would say) and, later, to San Francisco, where she made her home among the myriad poets she met there. As such, Lonnie was, simply by virtue of her existence, the first person to suggest to me that such audacious actions were possible. A young woman could move herself, alone, across the ocean. More importantly, she could order her whole world around the choice of words.

Lonnie's inspiration in my life only increased when she moved back to Michigan and into the Moscow farmhouse featured in this collection. She became my first writing mentor. I developed a deep respect for Lonnie's keen-eyed and whip-smart suggestions and, more than that, an abiding delight in her poems. I leapt at the chance to write this foreword simply because I wanted to linger over this collection in its entirety—over this long-ago woman speaking close to my ear, over this rich and resonant story of which I had read only parts.

The anonymous farmwife of Lonnie's collection lives a life constricted in its physical scope but limitless in its felt power, its staggering losses, and its depth of observation and experience. Lonnie interweaves the poems with a deft balance of particular and universal to such effect that the woman who steps out from its pages feels at times almost painfully true.

Lonnie's is an elemental protagonist stripped bare of superfluities. She is a woman who questions the ways of men. She is a woman who grieves the loss of her sister and of "her own girl, born too early." She is a woman who reaps an assuaging happiness from the natural world— from the round heads of flowers, the pinto mare, the sparrow's nest "made entirely of her own hair," the yellow tomcat who came to her "the day she forced herself out of bed...and put away the baby things." She is a woman who tries to hold her feelings inside, in a sort of reticule, yet sees them "pour out through the loose weave...like egg whites through her fingers/which later she will wipe clean and dry." And which of us has not felt this spilling, has not known this wordless language of grief or the consolations of beauty, has not questioned the ways of those who seem to move unshaken through the world?

Visually, Lonnie clears the landscape that surrounds the 1885 farmhouse. We see the pale stone slabs of graves, the "trillium sparking like stars," the white nightgown, the white birch, the white morning, the white flesh of apples, the white muslin bleaching in the grass. We see snow like "spilling lace" and blizzards that leave the hills "gleaming like milk glass," and always, of course, the moons. And across this pale landscape pop spare points of color that hit the mind's eye with an artist's power—the spilled raspberries, the yellow tomcat, the red clouds that "cluster like roses," the child's eyes "like warm molasses," the red-winged blackbird that returns to its post with an almost offending timeliness no matter what has transpired in the world.

The woman asks the question each of us ask when life has felt far too heavy for far too long: Is there meaning in this? Her world yields no immediate answers, but it does yield a quieting balm along with a whisper that arrives in her dreams. *Heaven is a comfortable place,* the woman's dead sister assures her, and in another dream, the woman's mother calls over her shoulder, *It's not how you think—/I am among the living/You are the one who's among the dead.*

In the end, it is the new lives that arrive in the woman's life that ease the pain of lives lost, and we come to hold the full heft of this truth—that beauty is connection, and connection is beauty, and our connections will restore us even after they have torn away parts of us that we can never retrieve.

In *She Calls the Moon by Its Name,* Lonnie has not only captured the post-Civil-War era in Moscow Plains, Michigan. Her journey into the interior of her protagonist is also a journey into the timeless interior of each one of us—into our unspoken pangs, our accompanying rhythms, our secrets and silent questions, and the scraps of beauty with which we piece together a life under a full and waning and waxing moon.

Michelle Webster-Hein
Author of *Out of Esau*

Moscow Plains, Michigan
1885

She calls the moon by its name

when she cannot sleep, does not
feel brave enough to name it herself,
even as it pales in first light. This month
the moon's name is *pink*, so say
the Potawatomi, and she wonders
if that is why today, as the sun
rises on her sleeplessness,
there is pink spread across the sky,
rosy pools against a gold cloud bank.
If these pink streaks were
lakes scattered over land,
she would never need to portage
to get from east to west. If they
were boulders in a creek, she could
cross over on foot and stay dry.
She rises to greet this sky, grateful.

Flower Moon

She is often alone

and yet, she is never alone
when the banty hens run to her,
when the foxes watch from the west field,
she knows, feels powerless to stop
the slaughter when it happens,
sees it in a whimpering dream, and when
she returns to clean up
the feathers and feet, the blood,
her own blood stirs inside her, the first
in so long that she buys more chickens,
and that is why.

She hopes with any luck
the lilacs will survive

this surprise snow covering the ground.
Her husband growls at the window: *Damned weather.*
You think you can read it, and it turns on you.
She stirs oatmeal, listens. He tells how
yesterday he left a baby bull for dead, then later
found it standing, licked to life by its mother.
He marvels at the cow's persistence with her newborn.
Already he has moved beyond
his disappointment in spring,
and she envies that about him,
that and other things.
She covers the oats and turns to the window
where red clouds cluster like roses.

She was born in the house, so was Lillie

and one by one the bedrooms upstairs
warmed for a time, then closed
and cooled, still filled
with cedar beds and washstands
for the occasional hired hand, and then
another room closed and another,
now the entire floor sits quiet.
She seldom goes up there, blames
her aching hip, but each spring
she makes the climb to open
those many windows for airing.
Soon enough, Walker goes upstairs
and closes them to keep bats out.
So he says.

Lillie always called her Sister

from the time Lillie could speak,
twelve years between them,
their mother forever tired.
On rainy days, they liked to play
Mary and Martha, those
New Testament sisters,
Lillie as Martha, truly
pretending, since never was Lillie
bound to a kitchen, not that dancing,
beaming, bright-eyed girl,
combs falling from her hair,
our morning star, their father called her,
a balm to their mother's sorrows.
Baby sister turned willowy woman
whom Asa wed, how was it possible
she could carry a child?
In the end, of course,
it was not, and there is
no balm for this.

She tends the graves

her mother's, her father's, all three brothers.
And on her own land, her girl, born and buried
twenty years ago. *You'll have another*, they said.
Her first, her only.
Now on Asa's land, Lillie and their baby boy.
She cuts yellow tulips that made it
through last night's freeze, why wait
for another killing frost, this spring
so oddly cold. A copse of locust trees
in fallow ground holds the single grave
of Lillie and her boy,
not even a cow path leads to it,
strange for a family plot, she thinks,
these trees meant for fence posts,
but then, this is Asa's first burial.
She moves toward the grave,
sees trillium sparking like stars,
then sees the headstone, there was
none before today and Lillie gone a year.
She feels the kind of dread she feels
when the hens are silent. It is as if
all this time, Lillie and the baby
were not really there under the sparse grass,
not until she sees this stone slab,
thin and pale like Asa himself,
the stonecutter's words shadowed grooves:
 My wife, my child
  It is well with them
She sinks to her knees.
Oh Asa, where are the names?

She finds she is angry

when she remembers Lillie riding like a man
on the back of a young black mare,
long white fingers gripping the mane,
eyes the color of dusk,
and when the reverend says
one day we all shall rise, and when
Asa says come get the woman things,
his voice frightened and harsh,
and when she thinks she sees Lillie
next to the tamaracks, when
she wills that image to come back, but it will not,
Jesus, she whispers,
oh Jesus, please.

She sees rain coming

like a pillar of smoke, gliding across the west field,
a cloud bursting-full, the air already
moist, pots of mint stirring in the window,
finches tucked away under porch eaves.
Wind rushes through the open parlor door,
knocks over the jar of tiger lilies
without breaking glass. Water drips
to pine floor planks. She pulls off her apron,
stops at the prone lilies, hand raised, recalls
the reverend's picture of the wife of Lot, the woman
who looked back, then turned into the salt
that begins to seep from her own eyes.
How could she not look back?

Sturgeon Moon

She bleaches muslin in the grass

the bolts anchored down with clean speckled rocks,
a hot dry wind billows it up,
mourning doves cry in the maples,
and when she hangs wet linens on the line,
the sheets sail up, then float down,
they cling to her sunburned skin, so cooling,
so good, she thinks of her husband on these very sheets,
surprised that she wants him again, remembers
how much she used to want him, maybe
for another baby but for something else, too,
how rosy her face grew watching him from the window
when he bathed his torso at the pump, how
she longed to touch his thigh during summer sleep,
holding back, such a sweet shame then,
now it's pleasure, maybe relief, and she hears
sheets snap in the wind, the trees creaking,
the soulful call of birds and remembers
her mother saying: *Mourning doves crying for rain*,
but she knows better.

She picks wildflowers in the afternoon

when the only sounds come from frogs, crickets, killdeer,
muted, banked in like fog, the ceiling of yellow sky
lowered, folding in around her in a kind of heat
people in southern lands sleep through, so she's told,
but not she, this is when she gathers her ladies—
black-eyed Susans, Queen Anne's lace—in a bucket
with shallow water, then sits under the catalpa tree
and tats her own lace, legs folded, feet bare,
the calico rolling at her knee and showing off
its amber belly, the pinto mare feeding on the lawn
with the gray tomcat sprawled across its back,
claws tucked in, a thing which delights the mare
who tries to nuzzle the tom, and at this time of day,
that pinto mare makes her happy, and it is enough.

The Book of Isaiah speaks of stones

She thinks so anyway, and she means
to ask the reverend about it, remembers again
when she sees overripe plums
drop from their tree full of wasps.
South of the stone smokehouse,
a black snake suns itself, lives
under the rotting corn crib, in that
skeleton of wood ribs spilling open.
She hears the bees hum, the clicking
of bats, smells the root cellar dirt
even from a distance, and beyond that
she sees fields full of round stones
that seem to sprout like potatoes
no matter how many they haul away.
She accepts these hard things of summer,
these dark spots, the bite and sting,
the heaviness that hangs on the heat
and seeps indoors each night, as quiet
as smoke, bringing with it a sadness
so familiar it borders on sweet. *Comfort ye,
comfort ye my people*, says the prophet.
But the stones are still hard.

She wonders at the ways of men

as she weeds the row of tall marigolds:
her father, a man of few words,
saying of her mother, *A fine woman
but unable to birth a living man-child,*
said the same way he might say,
Snow's in the southwest or
Lightning struck down the butternut.
She sees her mother after the third boy,
bed sheets black with blood,
legs crossed, rocking,
tearing at her hair, making sounds
she never heard before or since,
coming as she does from otherwise silent people,
and now here, squatting in the marigolds,
she wonders about her own girl,
born too early, how she wrapped the baby
in white linen, then watched Walker
bury her at the edge of the yard.
She tries making that noise her mother made,
rocks and listens until it sounds right.
She yanks the pins from her hair,
pulls on it hard, sits down in the dirt,
keens and pants, and it comes to her now,
to name her daughter-gone-away,
name her *Mary*, not
for the Madonna holding her own broken boy
but for the sister of the resurrected Lazarus,
she who sat at the feet of Christ, innocent,
that is her Mary, never to be

more than she was, and the name is good.
She speaks it, *Mary*, breathes it
among the marigolds, and the name comes easy.
She breathes slower, watches the sun climb,
gathers her hairpins in her lap.

She helps the congregation plant cedars

alongside the church, the closest they can come
to cypress, those stalwart trees that guard tombs
in the land of the gods. The reverend told of it
one Easter, he being a well-traveled man,
casting his net of word pictures. He spoke
of ancient temples built from white marble,
of blue water, blue sky, white-washed houses.
She looked out the window that Sunday
at pale fields, brown swamp water, a sky diluted of color.
This was her blue and white, this day, these people.
A memory of white linen. That day.

Locust vines wove a circle somehow

and all summer it drooped from a branch
over the milking lane, one perfect hoop,
fit for a dress hem. Now despite yesterday's wind,
she finds the circle still intact. She thinks
how much she likes round, always has:
bowls, plates, the rims of cups,
even chipped ones, a full moon,
her round oak table, even when
the sister-in-law with the brood of children
reminded her that a table with corners
can hold so many more,
and she wanted to say, *More what?*
but held her tongue.

Walker protects her from many things

but not the slaughters.
When he hangs deer from the sycamore,
their bellies sliced open,
she averts her eyes, makes
a wide arc to go milking.
Walker kills chickens for the table,
and he plucks them, even though
this is women's work.
Next time she gathers eggs,
she tries not to see
which hens are missing.
She fills her basket,
picks up her skirt hem,
moves on.

Corn Moon

She ventures across the road

for no particular reason, other than
sometimes she likes to see
what the house looks like from over there
by the north tree line, what a stranger might see
wading through broken corn stalks,
or a soldier, had the war been fought up here.
Walker always says their house
would have been commandeered,
made of brick as it is and on a main road,
twenty-six windows to all four directions.
She watches the house, and the house watches back,
its black windows like so many eyes,
the fields on either side of it
soft and flat like a quilt, so clean
no war seems possible.
When Asa came back from Andersonville,
too sick to eat anything but egg custard,
he told her it's so strange to stand outside a prison
once you've been inside it,
you might as well be looking at it from the moon.

The house smells like apples

their sweet dark fragrance
pulls the hired hands indoors.
She hears the men stomp boots in the mud room,
hears their deep chuckles when Walker says
he feels sorry for any apple that's not a Macintosh.
They move into the kitchen,
hats in their big red hands,
to three bushel baskets on the table.
She puts down her coring knife and begins
polishing an apple with a towel,
then holds it out, first one, then the next.
The men duck in deference as they receive.
She thinks of Eve as she offers fruit
to these shy men in her world,
men who only nod their thanks,
then bite into the red and yellow and white,
each time a sharp snap she finds
soothing in the quiet house.

At first she sees the fog as a shroud

settling over the fields of beans, but
she does not wish to start this day
with such a word. She could say the fog
is like muslin stretched over the mouth
of a jelly jar, or it could be like
the birth caul covering a newborn calf
before its mother licks it clean.
It could be like the clouds
in the calico's old eyes—
no, not that. Let it be the caul.
The bean fields, like a baby calf,
are born again this morning,
and the sun will lick them clean.

On the second day of fog, she goes to meet it

sits on the broad root of a broken down
apple tree, remembers being a child
in such fog, searching for fairy houses.
She hears movement in the grass,
keeps very still while the veil of haze
rises to treetops bronzed
by the burn of the sun. Slowly
horses and deer appear all around her,
they graze close together,
nosing fallen apples, until she forgets
this is still a fallen world.

She remembers the yellow tomcat

who came to her years ago,
the day she forced herself
out of bed to cook for Walker
and put away the baby things,
the day she went to the hay barn
after Walker left for the fields,
curled into a corner on the floor,
and breathed the raw living smells,
afraid to find hope in them until
that strange yellow cat walked in,
a big yowling male who crawled
right onto her lap and purred,
what was she to do but pet him
when he flopped on his back,
looking into her eyes like cats seldom do,
so she held him and rocked him, his heft
felt good in her arms, and for nearly a month
every morning after Walker left for the fields,
the big yellow tom followed her into the barn,
flopped on his back in her lap and purred,
and she held him and rocked him
while he looked into her eyes
like cats seldom do, how later
he would bathe his yellow coat,
lick away the wet salt of her weeping,
and when one morning he did not appear,
she chose not to worry, she chose
to believe that he simply took himself
to another woman.

She watches men burn the brush

in the north section, a fallow field,
where they say the soil's rich again.
Is it that way with people? she wonders.
Can you simply lie down,
maybe for a few years,
then one day find yourself
burning with promise?
Dandelion mornings returned?

She dreams in a new moon

She is walking down a cold starlit road, all ice and
shining, she minces along, slides along, sees the
curvature of the earth up ahead, black rows of crossed
fencing on either side, a small shadow down the road—
is it the baby girl grown up?—her breast-bone aches at
this thought until a voice she does not know reminds her
what she does know, that the baby is in the next life and
will always stay a baby, and the shadow grows larger as
she draws closer, it becomes the Potawatomi woman who
lives off Brown Road, her round face bright in the dark,
eyes beaming in the dark, they are deep, deer eyes, smoke
rises off her skin, no, it's steam, the Potawatomi woman
is so warm it's like approaching the sun, the woman does
not speak, simply radiates light and heat which melt the
road to a fragrant mud, as slippery as ice.

November is a cloak of many colors

lost in the smoke of a clearing fire
that stings her nose, waters her eyes.
She visits the graves in this haze,
leans on the family obelisk, hears
the amber leaves circling her feet,
their dry veins scraping on stone,
whispering in an unknown tongue.
She considers kneeling in those leaves,
but that seems like praying to the dead,
so she stays on her feet, moves homeward
following the scattered white of birches,
bright point to bright point, the flecked
white bark vibrating in the smoke, a thing
she studies while she breathes in, breathes out.

Wolf Moon
1886

She thinks she overslept

since the bedroom is filled with light,
but it's the moon, bright and round
like a giant Christmas orange behind wavy glass.
It wakens Walker, too, who proclaims it to be
the eye of God, then goes back to sleep,
but she doesn't like to think of God that way,
as a bold, bald, lidless eye in the dark.
She likes to think of God as a smiling old man
who lives on the hickory staircase in the hall.
She turns on her side, sees the stairs climb
to the empty rooms, thinks of Jacob's ladder
and that angel he wrestled for a blessing.
She imagines God himself sitting on her third step
dressed in a striped nightshirt, hunched over,
knees tucked under his chin. He casts her
a sideways look from under sleepy eyelids,
steady, kind. No need to wrestle at all.

Blizzards never used to frighten her

though they meant extra care,
the laying out of ropes from house to barn
to lead the snow-blind to milking and back,
bringing weaker animals into the kitchen.
She could say a blizzard took Lillie and her son,
since nobody could be called on to help
until long after Asa carried their bodies
to the back porch and covered them.
Snow made its way in, drifting
on the floor, on the quilt. That is how
she found them after the storm, after
the wind quieted
and hills gleamed like milk glass.
She wonders how many times
Asa visited the porch those days,
moving through clouds of his own breath,
the stomping of his boots muted.
She fears for Asa now, fears she will someday
find him hanging from a barn rafter
or burning down all he has.
She fears so many things.
And now blizzards too.

She dreams Lillie holds a bowl of raspberries

They spill down the white nightgown
Lillie always wears in dreams,
soaking it like blood. Lillie smiles anyway,
lifts one arm like a wing
and turns, moving barefoot
through a circle of rooms.
Her nightgown flutters around corners,
always slightly out of reach.

She sleeps with gloves on

the fingertips cut off, edges
singed from the wood stove.
This morning, tiny snowdrifts
line windowsills indoors.
She lights the stove, watches the flame,
then moves to the window. She sees
her breath, tracks the wash of first light
over stars, watches the way
the white of morning grows
brighter by the minute on tree bark,
the black branches, fence rails.
These snowy fields remind her
of clean bed sheets on a winter line,
stiff and white, until she sees
red spots in the snow
surrounded by a flurry of paw prints.
She moves back to the stove.

Sometimes it's best to figure a hard winter will never end

so that when it does, there's a thrill to the smell of green,
to the baring of skin. But not yet.
For now it's chapped hands and nothing but gray
in the sky, in the packed-down snow,
in her husband's hair, even more
streaking through her own hair,
which she brushes hard.
She knows but cannot see coyotes slinking outside,
their tails whispering over snowdrifts,
white-tailed deer huddled together like girls in church.
She thinks that if some animals didn't hibernate,
her heart would break like a mirror.
Where is the sun? Buried behind clouds.
Where is the garden? Buried under snow.
Still there.

Her father called it a kalb moon

waxing, not yet grown.
Lillie was this way, not new,
not full but so very bright.
She keeps Lillie's hairbrush made of bone
and still full of copper hair.
She remembers how
carrying the baby made Lillie's mane
so thick. Now late at night
when the moon won't let her sleep,
she takes the brush out,
pulls strands from it, inhales
a sweetness like August hayfields.
Her fingers work in the dark as
she tucks hair into an apothecary bottle,
caps it, then lays bottle and brush
back into the drawer.

She awakens startled

from a dream, this one so real,
Lillie holding yards of unfolded lace
spilling over her hands.
She slides out of bed in the dark,
recalls the blizzard dream,
the one where Lillie stood
in an empty room with long windows,
holding something else,
lips moving.
Days later, there was
the lace of snow covering the quilt
over Lillie's face, Lillie's hands,
nails broken like deer-bitten corn.
She wonders now about that blizzard night.
Did Lillie come to her?
Or did she rise up, hold her newborn close,
then burn through the spinning snow
straight to God?

They take the mare out in a February thaw

Walker warns her it will be cold,
but she goes anyway, leans against him
on the horse's broad back.
Pastures of snow melting in mud
look like bark on a sycamore.
They trot alongside a low sun
that casts their shadows long and flat.
She and Walker and the horse make
one silhouette, their movement chipping
stripes of light created by sun on bare trees.
They come upon the Kalamazoo River,
merely a creek here, and full
of broken, sagging ice. It's as if
something pulled out the river water
and chopped the ice into blocks
that now lean on each other in the hollow bed.
It confounds her, this creek, cracked
and broken like glass. This is not
the order of things as she understands them.
It makes her think of lightning in a blizzard
or the false spring that brings skunks
out of their dens, something
not quite right about it.
Something not right at all.

It was the day she stumbled upon a flock of wild turkeys

and they all flew up and away
except one tom who faced her
and spread his tail feathers
like the silk fan on her buffet.
It was the same day she found a sparrow's nest
blown from a yew tree by the wind
and made entirely of her own hair.
It was the day things turned for the better,
always she would see that day as
her very own dove holding green in its beak,
showing that the rain was done,
that there was dry land somewhere.

She bridles the mare to go visiting

The horse lumbers west to Brown Road,
takes a rocking step into a forest, then
a clearing. She finds the Potawatomi woman
next to a fire, silver braids to her knees.
In Algonquin, the woman's name sounds
something like Hosanna, but nobody is certain,
or maybe as Walker says, white folks
hear what they understand.
A hut made of mud has hardened
like a swallow's nest, it's covered
with birch bark and pelts, only old ones,
as this is a woman alone.
A thin dog and its fat puppies,
chickens, all wander in and out,
one mule grazes nearby.
Walker likes Hosanna's maple syrup,
trades for it sometimes. Once
he offered a milking goat, but the woman
didn't seem to know what to do with milk.
Wood smoke overpowers everything,
and that's just as well, animals living so close by.
Hosanna watches horse and rider approach,
reaches out to touch the mare's muzzle,
then squints up: *I dream a boy. He is you.*
The woman strokes the face of the horse,
then turns and moves without haste
back to the hut. The mule brays.
The mare snorts back, paws the ground.

She holds her feelings inside

sees them gathered in a purse,
a reticule with its drawstring pulled tight,
sees them pour out through the loose weave
like water through a colander,
like egg whites through her fingers,
which later she will wipe clean and dry.

She remembers Lillie petting the Belgians

as they stood teamed, large and regal, their harness
like the pelvic bone of an ox, the oiled leathers, noisy
shoes, blinders, *oh look, Sister*, she heard, and how the
duo tossed their grand heads, snorted, twitched their
ears, everything about them in motion, the alfalfa a
sweet dry fragrance, the sun, *oh Sister*, she heard,
don't they shimmer?

She dreams about a house with red and blue walls

filled with singing children,
and her dead mother,
who wears a checkered dress,
dances a jig from the old country,
all stoicism gone. The children
grab her mother's hands,
pull her into a circle, the walls
spin like a carousel, colors blurring.
The children's voices ring
like high bells and crystal,
and her mother, wet blue eyes,
calls over her shoulder:
It's not how you think—
I am among the living.
You are the one who's among the dead.

Worm Moon

When March roars in like a lion

ice crushes the cedars,
the deer take what falls,
and yet the air is sweet,
spicy sweet, even as
she still breaks ice for the horses,
as she braces against the wind,
as she waits for the lamb.

She sees the road as a river

that weaves from the east, bends to the west,
past the house and into the world.
Her uncle from the River Raisin
told her one meal each day
must come from his river—
a fish, a turtle, a bird,
anything that might rise from the water
and present itself. Now each morning
she wonders what sustenance
will her river bring?

She spies a red-winged blackbird

perched on a stalk at the edge of the cornfield,
the first blackbird she sees this spring.
It reminds her of Asa,
a loner long before the war.
She's always been grateful
Walker never caught war fever,
did not join his dreamer father
and Asa to march south. She remembers
seeing the men off at the depot,
Walker holding the reins of his father's horse.
At seventeen, he knew who would
raise his mother's children
and not for a season. Indeed, his father
dead within a month from influenza,
Asa home in '65, more silent than ever.
Even when word came that Mr. Lincoln was slain,
and they draped black bunting on the houses,
spring marched right down muddy roads,
flowering pear trees hastened into bloom,
the red-winged blackbird returned to its post.

Asa rides his horse into the yard

a dog trotting next to him.
She steps out to greet them,
Asa stays astride, looks at the ground.
Got to get me another bird dog, he says.
This one shakes at the sound of a gun.
He tells her he's had the dog since it was a pup,
it even sleeps in the house at night,
but he won't keep a gun-shy dog.
Got no name. No fleas.
The next thing she knows,
Asa rides away, and the dog is hers.
A skinny thing, shiny cinnamon coat
speckled like an appaloosa's rump,
big, splayed feet, gray eyes.
He looks up at her as if
she holds all the answers in the world.
Or maybe it's the venison stewing indoors.
The dog sniffs her apron, tail thumping.
She laughs and opens the door.

She hears an owl nearby

and feels a faint wish to see, but it's dark.
Calves in the weaning pen
bawl for their mothers
who cry back in the night.
A scarlet moon rises out of a hayfield,
bulbous, like a blister about to burst.
Is there meaning, she wonders,
in this red moon, the owl's hoot,
the calves' grief?
In the cobwebs she finds indoors
that she cannot reach or even care to try?
She allows the owl's song
to be her balm this night,
though it yields no answers.
She feels foolish for asking.

She watches a deer in water lilies

drink from the spring-fed pond,
a young leggy buck. Bright lily pods
float around his hocks
like messages on green paper.
One scar runs shoulder to flank,
white blaze of fur circles his nose,
uneven stumps at his temples.
He raises his head, sees her across the pond,
huffs at her, stomps his foot,
it splashes in shallow water.
She stays still until he steps out
to melt into the willows.
The water lilies tipple,
shift, settle down.

The reverend pays a visit late at night

He stands in the hallway, hat in hand,
refuses a seat, speaks directly to Walker:
It's my brother's boy. Six years old,
asleep in the wagon.
He tells how the brother was a teamster
raising his son alone in Battle Creek,
thrown from a horse, neck broken.
I have no wife, the reverend says,
though of course they know this.
No prospects of one, he adds.
I'm all the boy has. He stares into the dark.
So much in this world I do not understand.
He stops, seems unable to continue, though
it's hard to tell in the oil lamp's weak light.
Walker speaks. *Bring the boy in.*

Her heart leaps

She feels it, hears in her mind the words
leaps like an hart, words that belong

to the lame of the Old Testament
promised the happy grace of a deer,

and though she knows she is mixing words
that are not hers, they stay, become her own.

She cannot stop what rises and moves
inside her, what *leaps like an hart,*

oh, dare the red doe believe
her thirst will be quenched?

She fixes a pallet by the wood stove

the upstairs bedrooms too far away
for a child in a strange house.
They lay the boy on the quilts,
he is limp with sleep, curved into a half-moon.
The reverend strokes the child's hair.
His name is Seth, he says before leaving.
The dog slinks in and sniffs the boy,
flops down on the floor next to him,
sound asleep soon enough. She worries
the boy might wake up afraid.
All night, she rocks in a chair next to him,
dozing, watching the boy, the dog—
one, then the other, marveling
how two more living creatures
came to her, moved into her house.
She knows nothing of this child, only
his name and his black eyelashes,
so when he opens his eyes at first light
and turns his face full on her,
it gives her a start.
Eyes like warm molasses.
The dog whimpers in a dream,
the boy turns to it, he seems
not the least bit surprised.
He curls around the dog
and falls back asleep.

They whisper in the front room

so as not to wake the child.
Walker tells her he could use the help
a growing-up boy would bring.
He looks at her sideways
when he says this, and
she sees for the first time
how it's been for him all these years,
raised as he was, six brothers and sisters,
expecting his own house, this house,
would fill with children.
She touches his arm.
All these years.

Pink Moon

Adam named the animals of Eden

and Walker names his livestock,
but she hesitates to name anything,
not the chickens, not any creature
that will be slaughtered. She does not
name the dog, never tells anyone
that she named the gone-away baby.
It feels thrilling when Walker
whispers her name, but she will not
speak the name of the boy who's moved in,
nor does she say what he is to her,
what that word might be.
The angel told Jesus' mother
what to name her boy,
and God called Israel by its name.
Who is she to be so contrary?

She dreams Lillie stands in a field of ponies

and this time, Lillie speaks:
Do not fret, Sister.
Heaven is a comfortable place,
and I am never cold.
The ponies graze on vivid green grass,
they rustle around Lillie like toddlers,
the gray lifting its head above the others.
Lillie runs her fingers through the pony's mane,
then braids its coarse hair.
Silent again.

Walker stays home to nurse a sick heifer

so she takes the child to church alone,
sits near the back, unaccustomed
to having him with her.
She does not hear the sermon, hears only
the breathing of the boy next to her.
Afterward, congregants mingle.
She stands under a sycamore,
rests her hand on its scarred bark,
watches the boy play with others,
throwing, catching. He seems to know
not to scare the horses, but then,
his daddy was a teamster.
Across the road, a flock of sandhill cranes
stands still at the sounds of humans.
The reverend moves to her side,
they watch the boy in silence
until she hears herself say, *I'm afraid.*
The reverend sighs. These days
sorrow follows him like a stray dog.
He nods at the others, moves on.
For some reason and all of a sudden,
the cranes fly up and away, there must be
a hundred of them and so noisy.
The child stops his play to watch,
turns to her, waves.
Seth, she says, as if he could hear her.
She waves back.

Acknowledgments

Some poems from *She Calls the Moon by Its Name* have been published in the following publications:

Ariel XXIII—

> She wonders at the ways of men
> She bleaches muslin in the grass

ByLine—

> The Book of Isaiah speaks of stones

Current—

> She remembers the yellow tomcat

Driftwood—

> She calls the moon by its name

Dunes Review—

> She ventures across the road

Midwest Quarterly—

> They take the mare out in a February thaw

Paterson Literary Review—

    She tends the graves

Poem (U of Alabama, Huntsville)—

    She is often alone
    She remembers the yellow tomcat
    She thinks she overslept

Runes—

    It was the day she stumbled upon a flock of wild
        turkeys

The Small Farmer's Journal—

    She hopes with any luck the lilacs will survive
        (published as Lilacs)
    She picks wildflowers in the afternoon
        (published as Wildflowers)

Third Wednesday—

    November is a cloak of many colors
    She remembers her sister petting the Belgians
    When March roars in like a lion

Writers Reading at Sweetwater Anthology
  (Ann Arbor, MI)—

    At first she sees the fog as a shroud
    On the second day of fog she goes to meet it

Awards:

"The Book of Isaiah" speaks of stones received first place in *ByLine* magazine's competition

"She remembers the yellow tomcat" received Honorable Mention in *Current* (Ann Arbor, MI) magazine's poetry contest

Title Index

First Line Index

A

B